The BACHELOR

UNOFFICIAL COLORING BOOK

By Jenine Zimmers
Copyright © 2022

MOST FUN TO WATCH AWARD

She bragged about forcing her nanny to make her cheesy pasta and covered herself in whipped cream to impress Bachelor Nick. Corinne easily earns our award for most fun to watch!

BIGGEST COMEBACK AWARD

Ashley I. cried her way through Chris's season, and then cried her way through Bachelor in Paradise. But the girl rebounded big time when she married Jared. We'll still save her a box of tissues just in case.

PICKIEST BACHELOR AWARD

Brad Womack's claim to fame is giving NO ONE his final rose, despite a season full of eligible women. Even when he was allowed to come back and star as The Bachelor again, he couldn't make it work with the practically perfect Emily. Guess the journey isn't for everyone.

BEST BACHELOR QUOTES

NO. 10

"DEEP, INTELLECTUAL THINGS ARE JUST MY JAM."

– Olivia on Ben's season, working to establish herself as a Bachelor villain.

MOST INAPPROPRIATE AWARD

Rozlyn got herself kicked off Jake's season for an "inappropriate" relationship with a producer. She later denied the accusations, although we wouldn't blame her if she was attracted to a big … camera!

WORST
DINNER
DATE
AWARD

When Josh, winner of Andi's season, got to
Bachelor in Paradise, he tried hard to impress a new lady,
but could not stop himself from moaning through every
bite of pizza. #girlslikegoodtablemanners

BEST BACHELOR QUOTES

NO. 9

"I'M, LIKE, BEFUMBLED."

– Hannah B. on Colton's season, inventing her own vocabulary.

Shanae on Clayton's season made (even more!) enemies
in the house when she greedily helped herself to eight shrimp.

BIGGEST
APPETITE
AWARD

Krystal's baby voice on Arie's season was so intense,
you would have thought she needed a bottle.

HIGHEST
PITCH
AWARD

"IF IT'S A POMEGRANATE THEN GOD BLESS IT."

BEST BACHELOR QUOTES

NO. 8

– Ashley S. on Chris's season, rambling about an onion's layers before realizing she was holding a pomegranate.

THE BACHELOR
WORD SEARCH

```
A  H  X  G  L  T  Y  R  I  U  V  J  K  Q  P  G  X  S  Q
D  J  C  L  K  Y  X  E  N  G  A  G  E  D  G  E  Y  J  R
G  R  J  T  R  I  B  A  L  T  X  F  J  H  L  T  A  O  S
K  P  E  I  G  E  A  D  H  G  R  F  F  J  X  Y  D  U  C
K  T  E  W  E  U  T  T  A  F  T  G  F  K  I  P  G  R  J
L  A  E  R  A  A  O  G  S  S  Y  M  G  P  T  E  K  N  H
A  Q  S  L  S  R  P  B  D  F  H  O  A  T  R  O  K  E  E
M  C  S  G  I  Q  D  H  A  G  J  I  D  N  N  A  R  Y  D
P  B  U  H  C  M  H  Q  T  V  E  A  E  Q  S  S  P  C  S
T  K  P  A  F  L  I  C  E  B  F  K  S  C  H  I  M  T  H
G  R  A  S  T  I  M  N  A  H  F  L  R  B  A  O  O  Y  U
X  O  S  D  A  P  N  V  A  J  K  D  I  K  S  L  T  N  C
Q  S  F  C  H  R  I  S  I  T  J  E  G  R  D  I  G  G  A
K  E  R  U  T  L  E  T  O  A  E  J  H  U  W  P  X  P  M
F  C  O  F  H  K  S  E  G  S  G  D  Y  O  C  L  Q  O  P
D  F  P  F  J  H  F  J  T  D  F  M  W  S  G  L  R  L  R
S  P  L  W  U  G  T  F  H  F  D  O  S  E  X  I  I  E  O
A  H  D  R  A  M  A  T  I  C  F  F  E  F  W  H  N  J  P
B  X  W  O  P  X  B  C  M  V  S  Y  D  P  I  G  G  H  L
```

Words can horizontal, vertical or diagonal!

WORDS TO FIND:

Rose	Chris	Ring
Dramatic	Date	Engaged
Journey	Eliminated	Mansion

K

IS FOR KONFUSING?

WORST WITH NAMES AWARD

Before Jesse was the host of The Bachelor, he was the star of the show ...
and he once called out the wrong name at a Rose Ceremony.
Katie and Karen both start with K — words are hard sometimes.

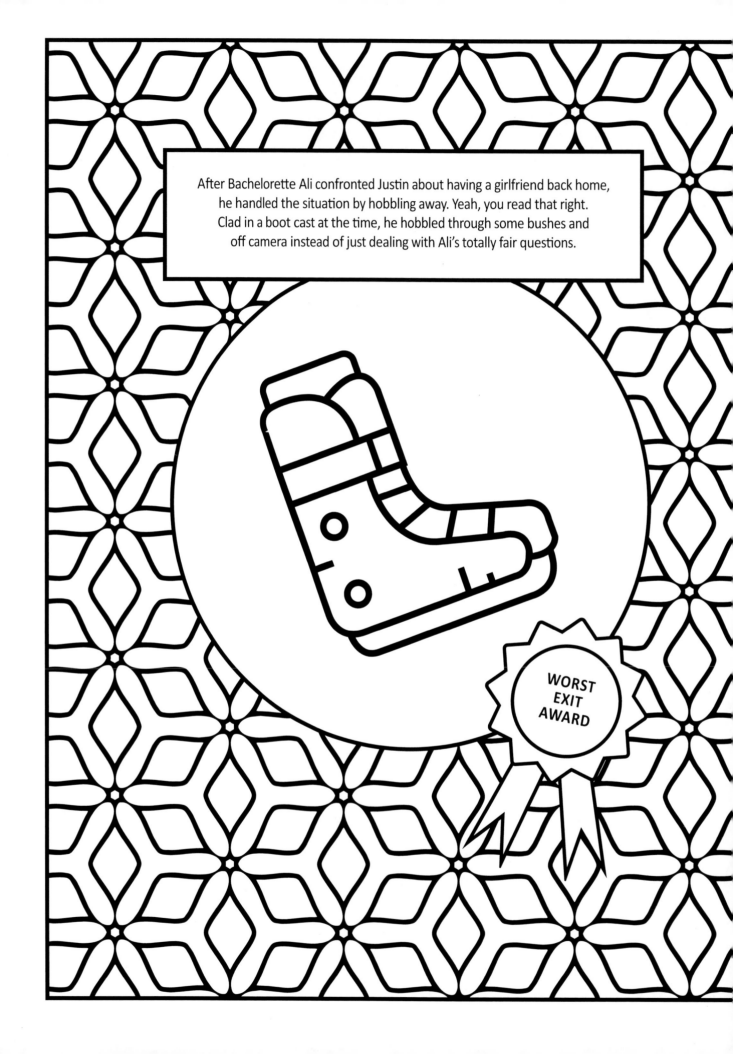

After Bachelorette Ali confronted Justin about having a girlfriend back home, he handled the situation by hobbling away. Yeah, you read that right. Clad in a boot cast at the time, he hobbled through some bushes and off camera instead of just dealing with Ali's totally fair questions.

WORST EXIT AWARD

THE BACHELOR TRIVIA

1. Who was the very first Bachelor?

2. Bachelor Travis Stork is now the host of what TV show?

3. Who was the very first person on the franchise to say, "I'm not here to make friends." (Hint: She was also the first person to be taken away in an ambulance.)

4. Where did Bachelor Chris propose to Whitney?

5. What year did The Bachelor first premiere?

6. Which Bachelorette contestant has been a runner-up twice and which ladies rejected him?

7. Which two Bachelorettes competed to become the star of season 11?

8. Which Bachelorette is now married to a former Bachelorette contestant's twin brother?

9. Which Bachelorette refused both of her proposals?

10. Which former Bachelor contestant was a bridesmaid in Jade's wedding to Tanner?

BONUS QUESTION: Where is the Bachelor Mansion located?

(Answers appear on final page.)

"I LIKE THE WORDS YOU USE. WORDS IN GENERAL. WORDS THAT YOU USE, HOW YOU SPEAK. SO PROPER."

– Bachelor Juan Pablo, paying a compliment to a woman.

BRUTAL BREAK-UP AWARD

After the "On the Wings of Love" season, Jake and Vienna ended their relationship on their very own – and very awkward – break-up special, in which Vienna sobbed while Jake yelled at her to stop interrupting. It was even more tense than a 2-on-1 date. Yikes.

"I CAN'T CONTROL MY EYEBROW."

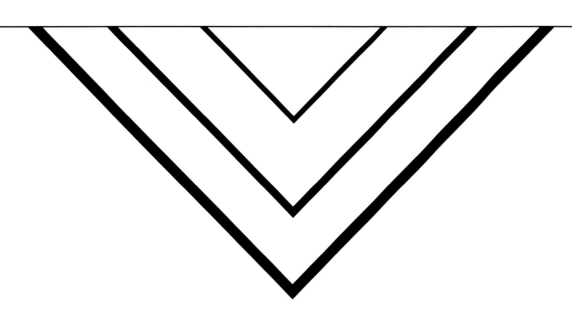

– Tierra on Sean's season, after other contestants complained she was making faces when they spoke.

"IT'S NOT OK."

BEST BACHELOR QUOTES

NO. 5

— Andi on Juan Pablo's season, letting him know she didn't appreciate his Fantasy Suite behavior.

MOST DELUSIONAL AWARD

Chad was a memorable Bachelorette contest who spent a lot of time drinking protein shakes and being unnecessarily aggressive. Oh, and he also ate a sweet potato like a piece of fruit. And threatened to cut off someone's arms, legs and torso. OK, bye!

The Bachelor Runners-Up Crossword Puzzle

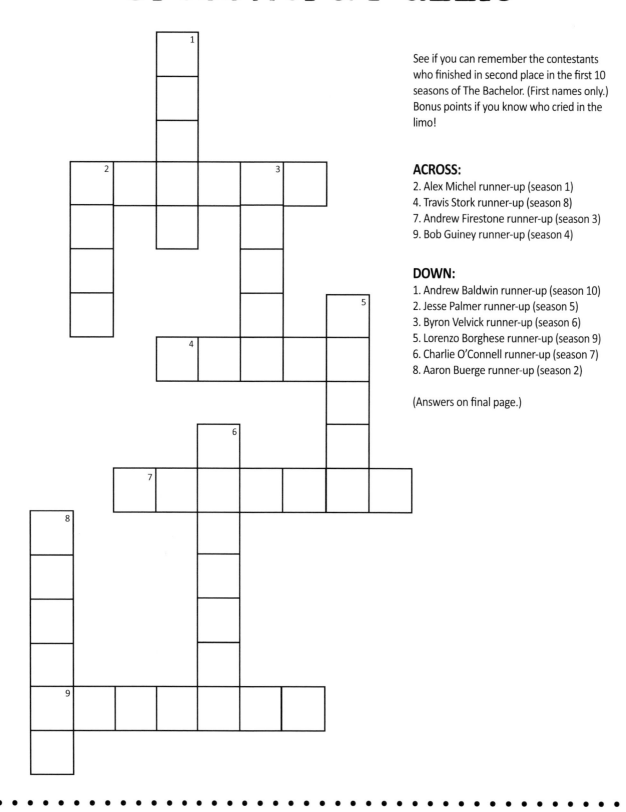

See if you can remember the contestants who finished in second place in the first 10 seasons of The Bachelor. (First names only.) Bonus points if you know who cried in the limo!

ACROSS:

2. Alex Michel runner-up (season 1)
4. Travis Stork runner-up (season 8)
7. Andrew Firestone runner-up (season 3)
9. Bob Guiney runner-up (season 4)

DOWN:

1. Andrew Baldwin runner-up (season 10)
2. Jesse Palmer runner-up (season 5)
3. Byron Velvick runner-up (season 6)
5. Lorenzo Borghese runner-up (season 9)
6. Charlie O'Connell runner-up (season 7)
8. Aaron Buerge runner-up (season 2)

(Answers on final page.)

While on Ali's season of The Bachelorette, Kasey got a wrist tattoo of a shield protecting a heart in order to impress her. He claimed he would guard and protect her heart forever. Or, you know, until he was eliminated, which he was shortly thereafter.

STUPIDEST GESTURE AWARD

Demi made a splash on Colton's season by kissing him right in front of the other women and not being afraid to speak her mind. At the reunion, when another contestant tried to shove a pacifier in Demi's mouth as a stupid joke, Demi threw it right back at her. And she continued to delight fans with her antics on multiple seasons of Bachelor in Paradise!

FAN FAVORITE AWARD

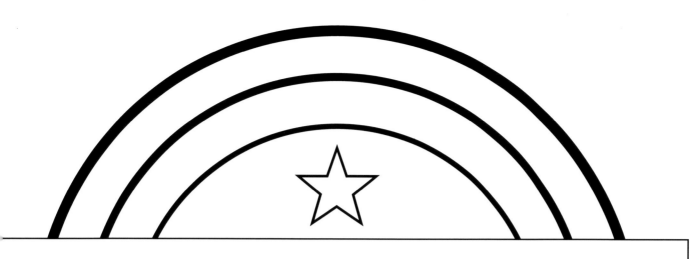

"MICHAEL JORDAN TOOK NAPS. ABE LINCOLN TOOK NAPS. WHY AM I GETTING IN TROUBLE FOR NAPPING?"

BEST BACHELOR QUOTES

NO. 4

– Corinne on Nick's season, defending herself after napping through a Rose Ceremony.

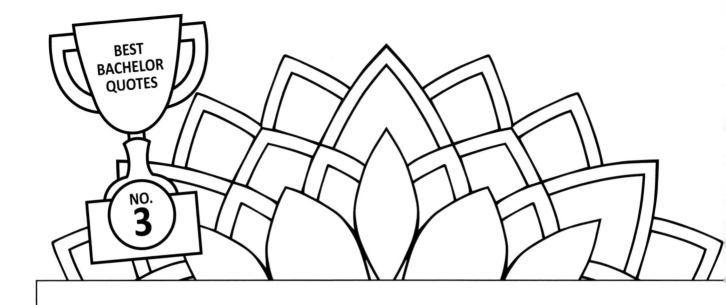

BEST BACHELOR QUOTES

NO. 3

"IT'S FROM EVERY WOMAN IN AMERICA."

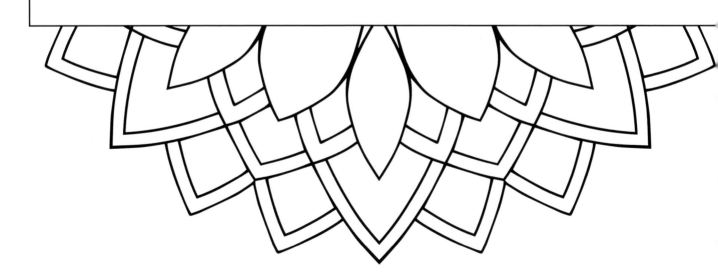

– Chantal, just before slapping Bachelor Brad as soon as she met him on his second season.

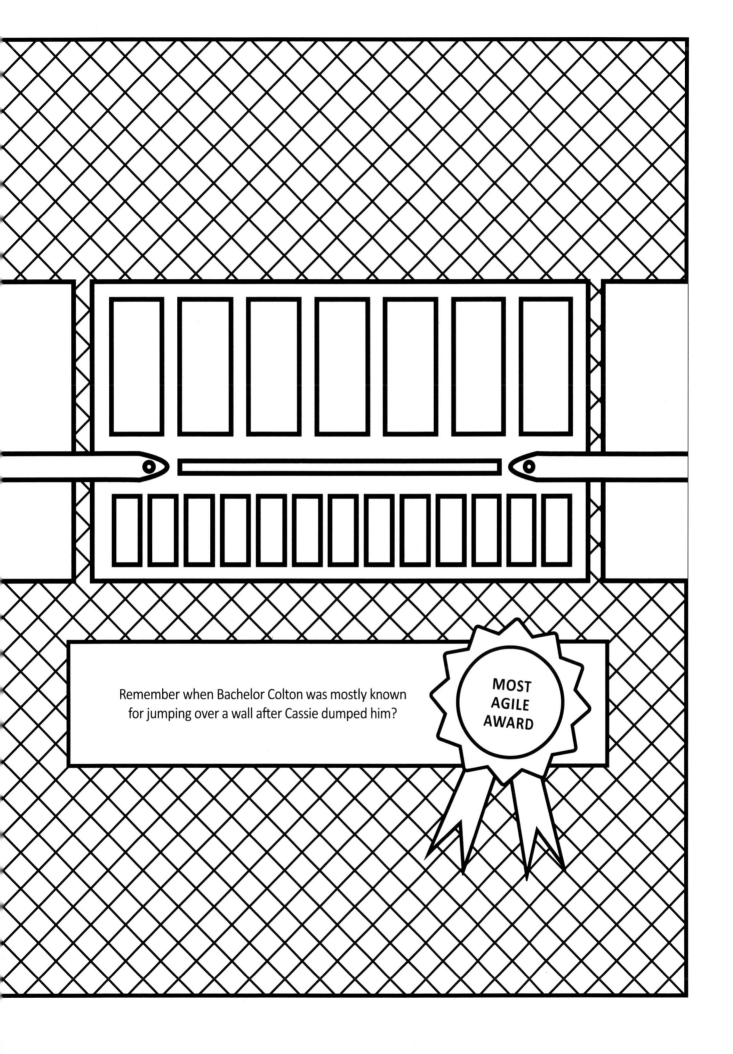

Remember when Bachelor Colton was mostly known for jumping over a wall after Cassie dumped him?

MOST AGILE AWARD

BACHELORETTE VILLAIN GAME

Match the Bachelorette with the villain from her season! (Answers on final page.)

1. Hannah	**A. J.J.** Claim to fame: Cared more about a bromance!
2. Becca	**B. Jordan** Claim to fame: Wore gold hot pants!
3. JoJo	**C. Kalon** Claim to fame: Referred to her daughter as baggage!
4. Emily	**D. Lee** Claim to fame: Totally inappropriate tweets!
5. Kaitlyn	**E. Luke** Claim to fame: Wouldn't stop talking about religion!
6. Ashley	**F. Bentley** Claim to fame: Bragged about making the Bachelorette cry!
7. Jillian	**G. Chad** Claim to fame: Threatened to cut off someone's torso!
8. Rachel	**H. Wes** Claim to fame: Was there for his music career!

BEST BACHELOR QUOTES

NO. 2

"I AM THE MOST IN LOVE WITH YOU."

– Bachelor Clayton, trying his best to explain how he can be in love with three women.

BEST DATE EVER AWARD

If you're a true member of Bachelor Nation, we don't need to explain this one. #fourtimes

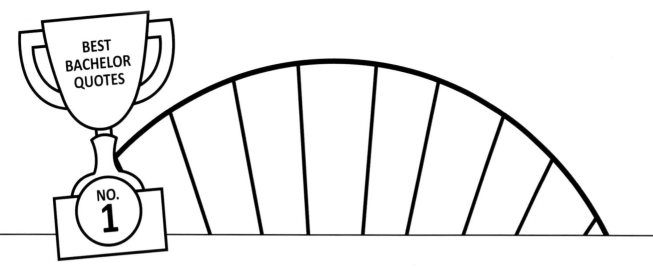

NO. 1

"WHAT DRAMA IS HAPPENING THAT I CAN JUST SIT AND WATCH?"

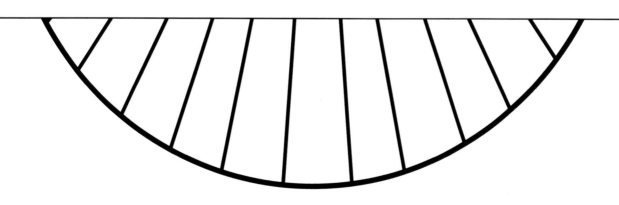

– Carly on Bachelor in Paradise, saying what we're all thinking!

The Bachelor Drinking Game

TAKE A SIP WHEN...

1. Someone says she or he "isn't here for the right reasons."
2. Someone says, "Can I steal you for a minute?"
3. You see footage of The Bachelor shirtless or in the shower.
4. The Bachelor/Bachelorette says, "I see my Wife/Husband in this room."
5. Anyone gets in a hot tub.
6. Someone says, "I'm not here to make friends."
7. Someone wears a ridiculous costume coming out of the limo.
8. Date cards arrive.
9. A date involves a helicopter ride.
10. A date involves a musical act or celebrity you've never heard of.
11. Anyone references a "physical connection."
12. Anyone references this being his or her last chance for love.
13. Anyone starts a sentence with "I could see myself..."
14. The Bachelor/Bachelorette says someone "really opened up."
15. The paramedics are called.

CLINK GLASSES WHEN YOU HEAR THESE WORDS ...

1. Amazing	3. Confused
2. Journey	4. Perfect
3. Dramatic	5. Process

IF YOU WANT TO OVERDO IT, DRINK WHEN ANYONE COMPLAINS ABOUT...

1. A group date.
2. Not getting enough time.

BONUS: Announce your favorite contestant the start of the episode. If he or she gets eliminated, finish your drink!

MOST DRAMATIC. SHOW. EVER. AWARD

Cheers to the contestant rivalries, the awkward 2-on-1 dates, and
the tearful limo rides into the sunset. We wouldn't watch without you, drama.
This is the final coloring page tonight ... when you're ready.

TRIVIA ANSWERS

1. Alex Michel was the first Bachelor.

2. Travis Stork hosts The Doctors.

3. Rhonda from season 1 was the first person to say, "I'm not here to make friends." (She also had a panic attack after getting eliminated!)

4. Bachelor Chris proposed to Whitney in a barn.

5. The Bachelor premiered in 2002.

6. Nick Viall was sent packing by Andi and Kaitlyn.

7. Kaitlyn Bristowe and Britt Nilsson competed to star in season 11.

8. DeAnna Pappas is married to a former contestant's twin brother.

9. Jen Schefft refused two proposals.

10. Carly Waddell was a bridesmaid in Jade and Tanner's wedding. (And Jade was later a bridesmaid in Carly's wedding to Evan!)

BONUS: The Bachelor Mansion is located in Agoura Hills, California.

MATCHING VILLAIN GAME ANSWERS

1. E

2. B

3. G

4. C

5. A

6. F

7. H

8. D

MATCHING VILLAIN GAME ANSWERS

ACROSS:

2. Alex Michel runner-up (season 1): Trista

4. Travis Stork runner-up (season 8): Moana

7. Andrew Firestone runner-up (season 3): Kirsten

9. Bob Guiney runner-up (season 4) Kelly Jo

DOWN:

1. Andrew Baldwin runner-up (season 10): Bevin

2. Jesse Palmer runner-up (season 5): Tara

3. Byron Velvick runner-up (season 6): Tanya

5. Lorenzo Borghese runner-up (season 9): Sadie

6. Charlie O'Connell runner-up (season 7): Krisily

8. Aaron Buerge runner-up (season 2): Brooke

Thank you!

The purchase of this book supported
a small business owner.

Made in United States
North Haven, CT
16 December 2022

28960343R00022